The Earliest Americans

Reader

Core Knowledge®

ISBN: 978-1-68380-109-2

The Earliest Americans

Table of Contents

The Earliest Americans
Reader
Core Knowledge History and Geography™

Chapter 1
Beringia: The Land Bridge

Ancient Hunters More than fifteen thousand years ago, huge sheets of ice covered much of Canada and the northern United States. In some places the ice was thousands of feet thick.

> **The Big Question**
>
> What was Beringia?

> **Vocabulary**
>
> **Ice Age,** n. a period in Earth's history when huge sheets of ice covered large parts of Earth's surface
>
> **land bridge**, n. a small strip of land that connects two large land masses
>
> **ice sheet,** n. a very thick piece of ice that covers a large area of land for an extended period of time

Scientists call this time the **Ice Age**. Much of the world's water was frozen into ice. There was less water in the oceans than there is today. Some lands that are now under water were dry. That's why dry land once connected Asia to North America. During the Ice Age, this dry land formed an area that scientists today call Beringia (/buh*rin*gee*a/) or the **"land bridge."**

Although there were no **ice sheets** on Beringia, the weather was very cold. At that time no one in the world knew how to farm. Even if they had known how, it was too cold in Beringia to

2

During the Ice Age, much of the world's water was frozen into ice, and the weather was very cold.

raise anything. Only tiny plants grew there. There were no towns, no stores, and no government, just a vast, cold wilderness.

So how did people in Beringia live? They had to look for plants and animals to eat. Small groups of just a few families, perhaps

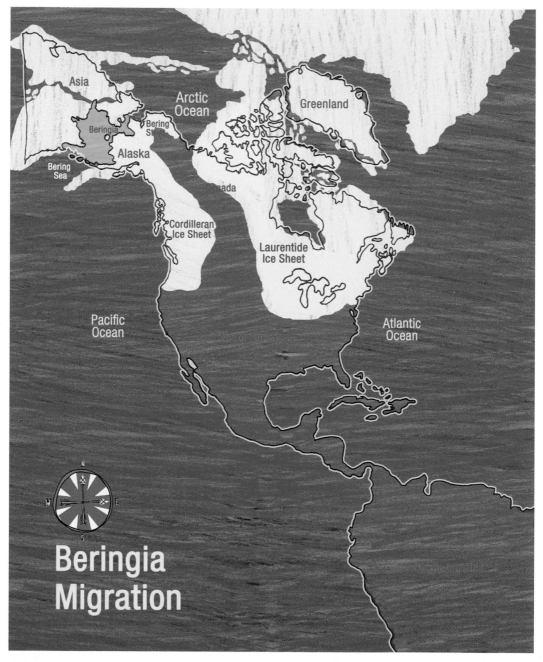

The ice sheets shown on the map were the two main ice sheets that once covered large areas of North America.

twenty-five to fifty people, helped each other as they moved around in search of food. People who live this way are called **hunter-gatherers**.

While the women and children of the Ice Age looked for plants and berries, the men and older boys hunted. They tracked **herds** of **mammoth** and **musk ox** back and forth across Beringia.

An Ice Age Boy

Imagine that you are an Ice Age boy in Beringia. You are hunting with family members, including your older brother, Tavalok. He learned hunting skills from your father and grandfather. Now he will teach you those skills.

Beringia is your home. But there are no maps, so you don't know that when you follow the animals toward where the sun rises, you are moving closer to a new continent—what we now call North America.

Searching for signs of a herd of mammoths, your group divides into smaller groups of hunters. In the distance you can sometimes see the other men, also looking closely at the ground.

You and Tavalok walk together, carefully looking for signs of the herd. As Tavalok crouches low on the half-frozen ground, you look back at the path you have traveled. The land rises up. The edge of the land and sky is lost in the snow and ice. Tavalok points to the ground.

Vocabulary

hunter-gatherers, n. small groups of people who feed themselves by hunting animals and gathering plants

herd, n. a large group of animals that live and travel together

mammoth, n. a large, prehistoric elephant-like animal covered with hair

musk ox, n. a wild ox with a shaggy coat and downward curving horns

Hunters shaped stones into sharp points that they attached to the ends of **spear** poles.

"See those footprints," he says. "We are going the right way. The herd has been following the wind."

You are carrying hunting tools, the snow is deep, and you are tired from carrying your

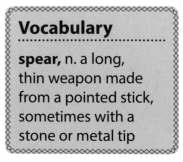

Vocabulary

spear, n. a long, thin weapon made from a pointed stick, sometimes with a stone or metal tip

supplies on your back. It has been such a long journey! You have never been away from your mother and sister for so long. They and other women and girls have stayed behind, gathering plants and berries for everyone to eat.

You trust Tavalok and want to learn from him. He knows how to read the sky. He can spot the animals' tracks and other signs of their presence. He knows where the land dips and turns. He knows where the ice ends and where the land turns to stone and dirt. He knows where to find plants.

After the group manages to kill one of the mammoths in the herd, Tavalok will guide you back to find the women and children so they can eat, too.

"Our shelter is this way," says Tavalok. "Come along now, little brother."

You hurry to keep up. Tavalok is already disappearing into the snow.

After a while you come to the place Tavalok remembers. Your legs are stiff, and your stomach is empty. You turn and follow the rock-filled river. Then Tavalok spots other members of the group. They have already built a fire. Soon all members of the group are back together again.

Because you are so far north, the light is dim, but it is not dark. It will not get darker during the night.

You eat the strips of dried meat you find in your bag. In the quiet glow of the fire, Tavalok shapes new spear points from stone. You imitate what he is doing.

The hunters made camp before continuing with the hunt.

"How far must we go until we reach the herd?" you ask.

Tavalok shakes his head. "How quickly does the mammoth herd move? I do not know. We will go toward the black clouds that cover the open land," he explains. "We will follow the tracks of the herd. I expect that after we sleep two or three more times, you will see the place where the rocks meet the sky."

"How far will the herd go?" you ask.

"It will travel to where the small plants and moss grow thick. We will not be far behind."

"And then will we be where the wind stops?" you ask.

"I do not think we will ever go that far, little brother," Tavalok laughs.

Early hunters followed the herd's tracks in the snow. Typically, they killed one herd member. For a band of twenty-five to fifty hunter-gatherers, one mammoth provided a lot of food.

Chapter 2
America's First Settlers

Who Came First? More than fifteen thousand years ago, Ice Age hunters in Beringia, like the ones in the story, were moving into North America. But many scientists believe that earlier people may have arrived thirty thousand years ago, by sea along the Pacific Coast.

The Big Question

How did the ability to grow food change the way people lived?

At that time, hunter-gatherers could not move very far into North America. Huge ice sheets blocked the way. About fourteen thousand years ago, the ice sheets began to melt. The Ice Age was ending. Hunters could now follow herds of animals farther and farther into North America. First they spread across most of what is now Alaska. Then they moved south, through what is now western Canada.

Between nine thousand and fifteen thousand years ago, groups of hunter-gatherers spread out through this new world. Little by little, they moved into the ice-free parts of North America. They walked everywhere—and traveled all the way to South America's southern tip!

Huron

Haudenosaunee

Cherokee

Creek

Seminole

Over a period of thousands of years, people spread over the land and settled on it.

A New World to Live In

By now the climate was getting much warmer. Water ran off from the melting ice sheets, carving out giant **river valleys**. North America's huge Great Lakes filled up. Melting ice water caused oceans all over Earth to rise. Many areas along the coasts were flooded, including Beringia. The rising sea cut North America off from Asia.

The various groups of people found two vast continents to live in and all the animals they could hunt. They continued to hunt large mammals such as the **mastodon**.

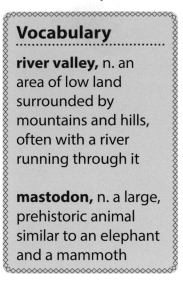

> **Vocabulary**
>
> **river valley,** n. an area of low land surrounded by mountains and hills, often with a river running through it
>
> **mastodon,** n. a large, prehistoric animal similar to an elephant and a mammoth

Over time, the climate changed, and this caused many large mammals to die out. The change in climate destroyed many of the plants the mammals ate. Overhunting the mastodon also helped to reduce its numbers.

Thousands of years passed. Groups of people moved from one place to another. As they moved, they learned to live in their new homes. They learned to use the resources available to them. They developed hundreds of languages. Their ways of life changed to fit the different parts of North and South America where they lived. Today, we consider these people Native Americans.

About seven thousand years ago, people in Mexico discovered how to plant and raise corn. Slowly, many other Native Americans began to grow their food. For many groups, the ability to grow food meant they could stay in one place for long periods of time.

In some cases, they stayed in one place permanently. In other areas, however, the climate or **soil** was not good for farming. In those places the Native Americans remained hunter-gatherers.

Vocabulary

soil, n. the top layer of Earth's surface where plants grow

The first corn raised by farmers in Mexico did not look anything like the corn we eat today.

Chapter 3
People of the Far North

The Coming of the Inuit People

Think about a frozen world. It is so far north that for six months of the year, there are very long periods of light. Then, for the other half of the year, there are very long periods of

The Big Question

What were the differences between life in the summer and life in the winter for the Inuit?

darkness. During the winter, it is very dark and cold. Moonlight gleams on the ice. The **northern lights** shimmer and arc across the sky. Stars twinkle, and their positions change as spring approaches.

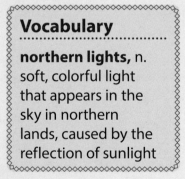

Vocabulary

northern lights, n. soft, colorful light that appears in the sky in northern lands, caused by the reflection of sunlight

During the Arctic summer, the sun does not appear to set. It does, however, dip close to the horizon, where the sky seems to meet the land. Even so, there are only about one hundred days when it is warm enough for water not to turn to ice. The warm season is too short to grow crops. But berry bushes and small flowers blossom.

This northern land has been called a "frozen desert." It is a hard place to live in. And yet it has long been home to an ancient group of people.

The Inuit moved from place to place while hunting.

The **ancestors** of these Arctic people came to North America about 2,500 years ago. Unlike Native Americans, they are not directly related to the Beringian

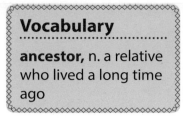
hunter-gatherers who lived at least fifteen thousand years ago. In Canada, the ancestors of the Arctic people are known as the Inuit (/in*yoo*it/). The word *Inuit* means the people.

When the Inuit first came to North America, they got almost everything they needed by hunting and fishing. They gathered plants during the short summer. Since there are no trees in the Arctic, the Inuit used driftwood. They collected the wood that floated on the sea or down rivers to make certain things they needed. They also made fishhooks, knives, and other small tools from bones and flint.

The Inuit built igloos as shelters when they moved from place to place while hunting.

About two thousand years ago, other peoples in northern Asia taught the Inuit how to make and use bows and arrows. The Inuit used these new weapons to hunt seals, **caribou**, and polar bears. Soon, knowledge of bows and arrows spread from the Inuit to other Native American people.

Living in the Arctic

A thousand years ago, the Arctic climate was a little warmer than it is today. Whales migrated along the Arctic Ocean coast. Some Inuit groups followed the whales east. They traveled from Alaska to northern Canada and all the way to Greenland. They set up villages. This meant they could stay in one place for more than a single season. On the sea, they traveled swiftly and safely in kayaks. Kayaks were canoes made out of animal **hide** stretched over a frame. The frames were made from driftwood or animal bone. On land and on the thick ice, the Inuit carried heavy loads on sleds. These sleds were pulled by a person wearing a harness or by a team of dogs. The Inuit became skilled hunters of whales and walruses. They used special tools such as harpoons tipped with bone, stone, and later iron.

The Inuit used dog sleds to carry heavy loads.

The climate got colder again five hundred years ago. It got too cold for whales to swim along the Arctic coast. The Inuit in Arctic Canada and Greenland could no longer live in one place all year. During the year they moved

The Inuit lived in small groups and hunted a variety of animals.

from place to place to find enough food to eat. They broke into small groups. They hunted smaller animals, such as seals. Some traded with Europeans, who were beginning to explore the Arctic.

A Year in the Life of the Inuit

During the winter, the Inuit crossed the ice to hunt caribou and seal. Some Inuit used blocks of snow to build shelters or homes called **igloos** (/ig*loos/). Families could live in an igloo. These frozen structures were sometimes connected by halls and tunnels. Families gathered to share stories, songs, and celebrations.

Vocabulary

igloo, n. a dome-shaped temporary shelter made from snow blocks

In the spring, the Inuit often traveled to inland rivers to fish for trout. As the ice melted, they could travel on the sea by kayak. Then, during the summer, tents made of animal hides replaced the igloos. The Inuit set up their camps on dry, high ground. Strong winds kept insects away. They used plants and berries growing on the treeless land of the Arctic for food, **fuel**, and medicine. Some traveled far from the coast in summer, hunting herds of caribou.

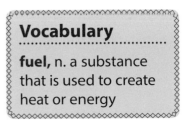

Vocabulary

fuel, n. a substance that is used to create heat or energy

In the fall, the Inuit returned to the coast to hunt seals, walruses, and whales. They built shelters near the coast. These shelters were made of rock-lined pits covered with earth. Families burned oil made from whale or seal fat for light and heat. They also used the oil for cooking.

Throughout the year, Inuit families stored as much food as they could.

Today, many Inuit live in communities that are more like yours. They travel by snowmobile instead of dogsled. Their kayaks are made of a light material called fiberglass instead of animal skins. They wear nylon parkas. But they also follow many of their ancient traditions. They understand the ties to the land, the sea, and the animals that helped them survive for thousands of years.

Each season brought about changes to how the Inuit lived.

Chapter 4
Ancestral Pueblo and Mound Builders

Meet the Cliff Dwellers It is late in the day. A young boy stands and watches the world around him. He is waiting for his father to return from a hunting and trading trip. The boy will be glad to see him.

The Big Question

How would you compare the settlements built by the Ancestral Pueblo to those built by the Mound Builders?

As the boy watches, he hears the rhythmic sound of his sister grinding corn for the evening meal. He hears his other sisters making baskets and decorating clay pots. His youngest sister sings with a clear, sweet voice that echoes through the **canyon** below. Maybe their father will hear her and hurry home.

Down at the creek, his mother fills the water jars. His little brother is there too, playing in the still water. The boy knows that in years when it rains a lot, the creek swirls and splashes over the flat stones. Also in wet years,

Vocabulary

cliff dweller, n. a person who lives on a rock ledge or cliff wall, such as a member of the Ancestral Pueblo people

canyon, n. a deep valley between mountains, cut through the rock by river water

The cliff dwellings were like small towns.

During the wet years, corn was plentiful.

the winter brings snow to the high country, where they live. Then the corn grows tall and the squash grows thick. The rooms where the food is stored are filled with jars of beans and baskets of corn.

Dry Years

But some years the winter snows and summer rains don't come. In those years, his parents worry whether there will be enough food for their village. When it's dry, his father worries he won't find many animals when he goes hunting. In the dry years, the animals move to places with more water to drink and more plants to eat.

The boy's grandmother is the oldest person in the village. She says that there have always been wet summers and winters with lots of snow—and also winters and summers when it was dry. But now she says that there seem to be more dry years than ever before. What is happening? The people don't know, but they are worried.

Now smoke from the evening fire curls through the upper rooms. The sky darkens. The boy knows now that his father will not return tonight. Maybe he had to hunt so far from the village that he camped along the trail. Maybe he has found a place where the land is rich and the water is clear, where the people can build a new home. The boy will have to wait for news. He climbs down a ladder to join his grandmother, mother, sisters, and little brother.

The young boy in this story lived one thousand years ago. His people were the ancestors of the **Pueblo** (/pweh*bloe/) groups that today live in an area called the Four Corners. This is where the present-day

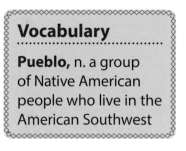

states of Arizona, New Mexico, Utah, and Colorado meet.

The boy's home was a village built into the side of a cliff, high above the stream at the canyon bottom.

Rooms were stacked on top of each other like an apartment building under the overhanging cliffs. Ladders connected the different levels of the cliff dwellings.

There, villagers went about their work. They wove clothing. They made sandals from strips of animal hide and yucca. Yucca is a southwestern plant with tough leaves. The villagers also made jars, bowls, and pitchers out of clay. They cooked squash, corn, and beans over open fires.

The Ancestral Pueblo

We don't know what the boy's people called themselves. The Native Americans who now live in the Southwest call these ancient people the Ancestral Pueblo.

The existence of the Ancestral Pueblo in the American Southwest goes back at least two thousand years. At first, they hunted game and gathered seeds, berries, and plants. Eventually, they began to plant crops near the streams in the valleys below the cliffs.

The Ancestral Pueblo were skilled basket weavers and potters.

The first native people of the Americas who raised corn lived in Mexico about seven thousand years ago. Over time, various groups of people in the Americas, such as the Ancestral Pueblo, also added corn to the crops they raised.

Because the Ancestral Pueblo raised crops for part of the year, they set up farming villages. As well as corn, they grew beans and squash. But they did continue to hunt and to gather wild plants. Women and girls had the job of raising crops and gathering wild plants. Men still mostly hunted and traded.

Ancestral Pueblo Villages

As the population grew, the Ancestral Pueblo spread over a wide area in the Southwest. They began building villages in several different styles, including the cliff houses like the one the boy in the story lived in. They made some buildings with stone or **adobe** (/uh*doe*bee/), which was made of clay. All of the buildings included places for sleeping and for storing food. They also had places for meetings,

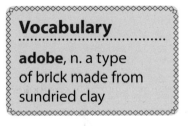

Vocabulary

adobe, n. a type of brick made from sundried clay

religious ceremonies, and celebrations. Outdoor plazas or porches connected the living areas. One style of building was two or three stories high. The flat roof of one story formed the porch for the story above. Ladders connected each level.

The Ancestral Pueblo also built paths and trails to connect the settlements where they lived. With other groups, they traded pottery, woven goods, jewelry, and tools.

What Happened to the Ancestral Pueblo?

For hundreds of years, the Ancestral Pueblo lived as cliff dwellers in an area of the Four Corners. Suddenly, they were gone. What happened? We don't know. Scientists have several different ideas.

Farming can be very hard. Plants need light, warmth, and water to grow. They also need **minerals** in the soil to be healthy. Over many years, the Ancestral Pueblo may have worn out the soil.

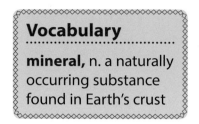

Vocabulary

mineral, n. a naturally occurring substance found in Earth's crust

The weather also may have changed. Without enough rainfall, it is difficult to grow food to eat. The animals used for food struggle to survive, too.

No one knows for sure why the Ancestral Pueblo left.

Something made the Ancestral Pueblo leave their cliff dwellings and move. We may never know exactly what it was. Today, the Pueblo people who live in small groups throughout the Southwest trace their roots to the Ancestral Pueblo, the cliff dwellers of long ago.

The Mound Builders

Just as the Ancestral Pueblo did, other ancient Native Americans learned to live in a way that seems very mysterious to us today. One such group of people was called the **Mound** Builders. They once lived near rivers in what is now the Midwest and in the Southeast. Their way of life began about 2,800 years ago. This was about the same time as the civilization of ancient Greece.

> **Vocabulary**
>
> **mound,** n. a large, rounded pile

Like the Ancestral Pueblo, the Mound Builders were farmers. They grew corn, squash, and beans. Because they were farmers, the Mound Builders settled in one place. They raised so much food they could trade with other groups. They built cities, roads, and marketplaces.

Building a Town

Let's watch the Mound Builders as they build a town. Using baskets, they collect dirt and heap it up into huge piles to form flat-topped mounds. The tallest mounds are several stories high! Then they put buildings on top of the mounds. The buildings might be temples or houses.

The Mound Builders' villages stretched along the Mississippi River Valley. Their villages spanned from the present-day states of Ohio, Wisconsin, and Minnesota to Louisiana and the southeastern United States.

What happened to the Ancestral Pueblo cliff dwellers is still a mystery. We do, however, know what happened to some of the Mound Builders. The cities of the Mound Builders lasted for hundreds of years. During this time some groups of Mound Builders became very powerful, while others fell from power. Then came the arrival of European explorers in the 1500s. The people of the Mississippi Valley could not fight off the germs and diseases carried by the Europeans. In a very short time, they began to die rapidly.

Survivors of the Mound Builders became the Native American nations known today as the Creek, the Cherokee, and the Choctaw. In the late 1600s, French explorers saw the last Mound Builder city in what is now Mississippi. It was ruled by a wealthy, powerful king. But by the early 1700s, this city was gone, too.

The Mound Builders used piles of dirt to build mounds of different sizes.

The community held ceremonies, meetings, and games in a central plaza. The most respected and most important people in the village lived on the tallest mounds, close to the plaza.

Chapter 5
After the Ancestral Pueblo

The Pueblo Native people and scientists agree that the descendants of the Ancestral Pueblo cliff dwellers include the Pueblo. Today, these people live in the American Southwest.

The Big Question
....
What are some of the reasons why some Native American groups moved from place to place?

In Spanish, the word *pueblo* means village. In the 1500s and 1600s, the first Spanish explorers arrived in the Southwest. There they met the native people. The Spanish named these people for the villages where they had lived and farmed for hundreds, even thousands, of years.

Pueblo villages look like they're modeled after Ancestral Pueblo cliff dwellings. Like the Ancestral Pueblo, the Pueblo built apartment-style homes out of adobe bricks.

This is one reason scientists feel certain that the Pueblo people are related to the ancient Ancestral Pueblo cliff dwellers.

One group of Pueblo people named the Hopi built their villages on the tops of mesas for protection from enemy attacks.

Like the ancient Ancestral Pueblo, the Hopi built homes with different levels connected by ladders.

Nineteen Pueblo villages still exist. They can be found on the high **mesas** (/may*sahs/), in the deep canyons, and along the river valleys of New Mexico. All Pueblo villages share many traditions

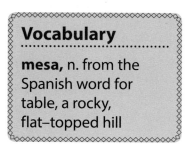

Vocabulary

mesa, n. from the Spanish word for table, a rocky, flat–topped hill

passed down from their ancestors. But each separate village also has its own special customs.

The Hopi and the Zuni

The Hopi (/hoe*pee/) are Pueblo people. They stayed in the high desert or on the plateau areas of Arizona, just like their ancestors. They built villages on the high mesas. There they grew corn, squash, beans, and melons. The word *Hopi* comes from a phrase that means the peaceful people. Today, the Hopi live mostly in northeastern Arizona.

The Zuni (/zoon*ee/) are also Pueblo. They live in the western part of New Mexico. The Zuni do not share a language with the other Pueblo groups.

The Navajo

For tens of thousands of years, groups of Native Americans have migrated. Some moved to follow **game**. Some moved because the climate changed. Some moved to find more or better land. Others were driven away by enemies. Whenever people move, they bring some things with them. They leave other things behind.

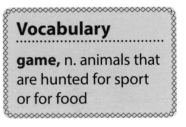

Vocabulary

game, n. animals that are hunted for sport or for food

The Navajo (/nah*vah*hoe/) migrated from northern Canada to the Southwest. In their language, they call themselves Diné (/dih*nah/), meaning the people. The Navajo language links them to their ancestors in Alaska and Canada. Perhaps the Navajo are directly related to the hunter-gatherers who lived in Beringia many thousands of years ago.

The Navajo who came to the Southwest from Canada fought with the Pueblo who had lived in the Southwest for thousands of years. But the Navajo also learned from the Pueblo. They learned how to survive in the harsh climate of the high desert. For example, the Navajo often used adobe to build their homes. But they built individual domed houses in small, scattered groups, rather than in villages.

The Spanish first brought sheep to the Southwest in the 1600s. As a result, raising sheep became a big part of the Navajo way of life. The Navajo became more settled. They used fleece from their sheep to spin wool and weave blankets and rugs. Still known for their weaving skills, today the Navajo make up the largest Native American nation in the United States.

After being introduced by the Spanish, sheep became an important part of Navajo life.

The Apache and the Comanche

Like the Navajo, the Apache (/uh*pach*ee/) also migrated from northern Canada to the Southwest. They traveled along the eastern side of the Rocky Mountains. Apache territory covered parts of present-day Texas, New Mexico, Arizona, and northern Mexico.

The Apache hunted and traded. Later, after the Spanish brought horses to America, the Apache learned how to ride the new animals. Horses made it easier for the Apache to hunt and to raid rival Navajo villages, as well as to attack Spanish forts.

The Spanish introduced horses to the Americas, and the Apache learned to use these new animals. The Apache hunted on horseback. They used buffalo hides to make tepees.

The Comanche (/kuh*man*chee/) were the only Native Americans more powerful than the Apache. The Comanche successfully gained Apache land and pushed the Apache farther west. Because of this, the Apache finally had to make peace with their enemies, the Spaniards. They needed Spanish protection from the Comanche. On a hot summer's day in the 1700s, four Apache chiefs and their followers met with Spanish missionaries in San Antonio, Texas. There the Apache turned over their weapons. In a ceremony of peace, the Apache and the Europeans "buried the hatchet." This meant that they agreed to stop fighting with each other. We still use the expression "bury the hatchet" when we agree to stop arguing with someone.

The horse was important to the Apache and to the Comanche.

Unfortunately, the "hatchet" wasn't really "buried." Not all the Apache made peace. Nor did the Europeans or their descendants leave them alone. All through the 1800s, the Apache were at war with other Native Americans and with various settlers. They fought against the Spaniards, the Mexicans, and finally the Americans. One of the most famous Apache leaders was Geronimo, who fought to save his people's land.

Today several Apache groups live in the southwestern United States. The Comanche mostly live in Oklahoma.

Chapter 6
After the Mound Builders

The Creek Nation As you know, the Mound Builders' way of life ended in the 1500s and 1600s. This happened when Europeans and the germs they carried spread through what is now the southern United States.

The Big Question

What were the key characteristics of the Creek, Seminole, and Cherokee Nations?

Vocabulary

confederacy, n. a loosely organized group of states or tribes

Mound Builder survivors probably joined other Native American groups in this region who lived in villages and small towns. Some of these groups became the Creek **Confederacy**, along the Mississippi River.

The Creek Nation formed after the Mound Builder culture broke up, sometime before 1600. Creek communities were a lot like the Mound Builder communities.

Creek villages were similar to the communities built by the Mound Builders.

The Creek kept parts of Mound Builder culture. Creek towns had a plaza for ceremonies and games. They had a house where the **council** met. The chief and the assistant chief lived on the plaza.

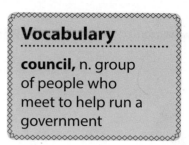

Vocabulary
....

council, n. group of people who meet to help run a government

Most members of the Creek Confederacy spoke the same language. They held the same religious ceremonies. When a town got too big, part of the group would split off and start a new town nearby. In this way, the Creek spread into North and South Carolina, Georgia, Florida, Alabama, Mississippi, and Louisiana.

Creek towns and villages were well-planned. Cattle, hogs, and other livestock were kept in fenced areas. Corn and potatoes were grown on farmland between the villages.

Creek people also lived in small settlements, or villages, near larger settlements, or towns.

The Seminole

Members of the Seminole (/sem*uh*nole/) Nation are also descended from the Mound Builders. They live in present-day Florida and Oklahoma. Every Seminole is a member of one of eight **clans**, or family groups. The clans are named Bear, Deer, Wind, Bigtown, Bird, Snake, Otter, and Panther. The Panther clan is the largest.

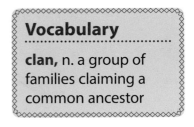

Vocabulary

clan, n. a group of families claiming a common ancestor

Members of animal clans believe that they are related to these animals. They believe these animal ancestors taught their clan how to live. People belong to their mothers' clans.

The Cherokee

The Cherokee (/chair*uh*key/) are another southeastern people descended from the Mound Builders. Their homeland was in western North Carolina, eastern Tennessee, and northern Georgia. Some Cherokee still live there. Sadly, most of the Cherokee and many Seminoles were forced to move from their homeland to what is now Oklahoma.

Like other southeastern Native Americans, the Cherokee lived in small communities on good farming land. They built wood-frame houses with walls made of woven vines or branches plastered with mud. Each village had a central building, or council house, for celebrations, ceremonies, and meetings. This council house had seven sides. Each side represented one of the Cherokee clans. The clans were Bird, Paint, Deer, Wolf, Blue, Long Hair, and Wild Potato.

The Cherokee lived in small farming communities.

Each group of Cherokee had two chiefs. One chief ruled during peacetime. The other chief ruled during war. The chiefs helped to guide the people and make decisions. But the chiefs did not have complete control over the people. The people had a say in how they were ruled.

Like all other Native American people, the Cherokee told many legends. These legends explained how their world had come into being and how people should live. In the late 1700s and early 1800s, the Cherokee became the only Native American people in the United States who also kept written records.

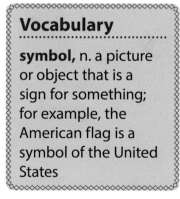

Vocabulary

symbol, n. a picture or object that is a sign for something; for example, the American flag is a symbol of the United States

Sequoyah

The written language of the Cherokee was created by a man named Sequoyah (/si*kwoi*uh/). He was born in the 1770s in Tennessee. Sequoyah became interested in books and letters, which he had seen written in English. He invented a set of **symbols** for the Cherokee language. This allowed the Cherokee language to be written and read. Sequoyah's work was a great achievement.

Cherokee Alphabet

D a	R e	T i	Ꮠ o	Ꮎ u	i v
S ga Ꭺ ka	Ꮇ ge	Ꭹ gi	A go	J gu	E gv
Ꮖ ha	Ꭾ he	Ꭰ hi	Ꮊ ho	Ꮍ hu	Ꮏ hv
W la	Ꮳ le	Ꮅ li	Ꮄ lo	M lu	Ꮙ lv
Ꮨ ma	Ꮝ me	H mi	Ꮔ mo	Ꭹ mu	
Ꮎ na Ꮏ hna G nah	Ꮕ ne	Ꮗ ni	Z no	Ꮗ nu	Ꮕ nv
Ꭲ qua Ꮝ s	Ꮖ que	Ꮖ qui	Ꮵ quo	Ꮝ quu	Ꮖ quv
Ꮜ sa Ꮝ s	Ꮞ se	Ꮏ si	Ꮩ so	Ꮖ su	Ꮢ sv
Ꮣ da Ꮤ ta	Ꮥ de Ꮧ te	Ꮧ di Ꮨ ti	Ꮩ do	Ꮪ du	Ꮣ dv
Ꮫ dla Ꮬ tla	Ꮮ tle	Ꮯ tli	Ꮰ tlo	Ꮱ tlu	Ꮲ dv
Ꮳ tsa	Ꮴ tse	Ꮵ tsi	Ꮶ tso	Ꮷ tsu	Ꮸ tsv
Ꮹ wa	Ꮺ we	Ꮻ wi	Ꮼ wo	Ꮽ wu	Ꮾ wv
Ꮿ ya	Ᏸ ye	Ᏹ yi	Ᏺ yo	Ᏻ yu	B yv

Sounds represented by vowels.

a as a in father or short as a in rival   o as aw in law or short as o in not
e as a in hate or short as e in met   u as oo in fool or short as u in pull
i as i in pique or short as i in pit   v as u in but, nasalized.

Consonant Sounds.

g nearly as in English, but approaching to k. d nearly as in English, but approaching to t. h k l m n q s t w y, as in English.
Syllables beginning with g except Ꭷ have sometimes the power of k. Ꭰ.Ꭶ.Ꮝ are sometimes sounded to tu, tv, and syllables written with tl,
except Ꮮ. sometimes vary to dl. _____

Sequoyah created a system for writing the Cherokee language.

43

Chapter 7
The Eastern Woodlands

Living in the Woodlands By the time Columbus landed in 1492, many different native peoples were living in the Eastern Woodlands of North America. The Eastern Woodlands stretched from Lake Superior to the Atlantic Coast.

The Big Question

What was the purpose of the Haudenosaunee Confederacy?

Vocabulary

landscape, n. the physical features of an area

The **landscape** of the Eastern Woodlands was mostly forest. Most people lived in clearings near creeks, rivers, lakes, or ponds between forested areas. There was plenty of wood for building and for fuel. There were many big and small animals and birds to hunt. There was almost a year-round supply of fish. There were a lot of roots, berries, and nuts to collect.

The Three Sisters

Besides all of the food that was available just outside the door, the land could be cleared in order to plant crops. The soil was rich, even though in some areas the growing season was short. Corn, beans, and squash were the main crops.

The Haudenosaunee lived in longhouses.

Corns, beans, and squash were grown together and called "the three sisters."

One Eastern Woodlands people, the Haudenosaunee (/hoe*den*o*saw*nee/), called these main crops "the three sisters." All three crops were planted together.

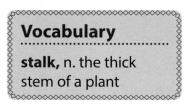

Vocabulary

stalk, n. the thick stem of a plant

Corn seeds were planted in rows of little hills, one step apart. Beans were planted between the corn plants. The beans could climb up the corn **stalks** as they grew taller. Squash was grown in the low areas between the hills. The broad leaves of the squash plants provided shade to stop weeds from growing. The squash plants also kept the ground moist.

Wigwams and Longhouses

The Eastern Woodlands people lived in small villages. They built their houses out of forest materials. Around the Great Lakes,

Eastern Woodlands people who lived near the Great Lakes lived in wigwams.

people built **wigwams**. A wigwam had a framework of poles pounded into the ground in a circle. The poles were tied together at the top to make a dome. Bark, reeds, or mats were used for the walls. Fires were built in the middle of the floor. Smoke escaped through a hole at the top.

The Haudenosaunee didn't live in wigwams. They lived in **longhouses**. These were also built with wooden poles. The houses formed a long rectangle with

Vocabulary

wigwam, n. a domed dwelling made of poles tied together with bark covering the sides built by the Eastern Woodlands people

longhouse, n. large, rectangular dwelling with doors located at each end and places for fires inside

a door at each end. There were fire pits in the center of the room. Smoke escaped through holes in the roof. Longhouses were about twenty feet wide. They could be long or short, depending on how

A longhouse could hold as many as ten families.

many families lived in the building. A typical longhouse held ten families with five fire pits.

The Mahican

Another group of Eastern Woodlands Native Americans was the Mahican. Their name comes from *muh-he-cn-nuk,* meaning great water that is always moving, either flowing

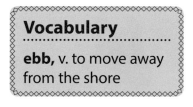

Vocabulary

ebb, v. to move away from the shore

or **ebbing**. Stories passed down for many years tell about the Mahican crossing over the water that gave them their name. This water, said the legend, was far in the north. There, two lands were nearly connected. Then the Mahican traveled east. They crossed many rivers. Finally, they found a place that seemed like home. It was the valley of the Hudson River.

The Mahican spent years fighting against neighboring nations. The Mohawk were their bitterest enemies. Both groups became great fighters because of their constant battles with each other!

The Haudenosaunee Confederacy

In the 1500s, there was plenty of food, but not very many people in the rich woodlands of the Northeast. Still, the Woodlands nations quarreled among themselves. They needed to find a way to stop the fighting.

Five nations formed a confederacy, the Haudenosaunee Confederacy. Most of the nations who joined the confederacy lived in what is now New York State. The nations were the Mohawk, the Onondaga (/ah*non*dah*guh/), the Seneca (/se*nih*kuh/), the Oneida (/oe*ny*duh/), and the Cayuga (/kay*yoo*gah/).

They did this to keep the peace among themselves and unite against enemies. One by one, each chief, or **sachem** (/sah*chum/), agreed to the plan. They knew their survival depended on cooperation.

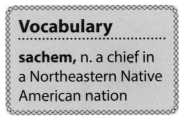

Vocabulary

sachem, n. a chief in a Northeastern Native American nation

The confederacy discussed problems and found solutions at council meetings. It also had its own laws.

All adults—men and women—had a voice in making decisions. The women were very good farmers. They produced much of the food that the Haudenosaunee ate. As a result they had a major voice in tribal meetings.

Haudenosaunee leaders discussed common problems in council meetings.

Haudenosaunee men were mighty warriors. They were feared by their Native American and French enemies.

It is sometimes said that the Haudenosaunee Confederacy influenced the contents of the United States Constitution. Even so, several Eastern Woodlands nations, including the Haudenosaunee, sided with the British during the American Revolution. When the United States gained its independence, it was a serious defeat for the Haudenosaunee. They could no longer expect help from the British. They had to try to stop thousands of settlers from seizing their lands on their own.

The strength of the Haudenosaunee Confederacy greatly impressed many people. Some confederacy ceremonies became famous throughout North America. For example, the confederacy's council meetings were called to order by the smoking of a pipe. The saying "smoking the **peace pipe**" comes from this tradition. Like "burying the hatchet," "smoking the peace pipe" has become part of our everyday language. It means sitting down and calmly talking over a problem to reach a fair solution.

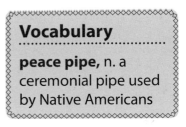
A Sad Struggle Between Peoples

One sad part of American history is the struggle between European Americans and Native American peoples. Their ways of life were completely different. European Americans wanted to take the land for farms. Native Americans got their food by hunting and gathering over large areas or by farming on small amounts of land.

Losing huge amounts of land to settlers meant giving up their traditional way of life. Many Native Americans fought until they were defeated or driven away. Many others died of diseases that Europeans brought with them. Unfortunately, ways could not be found to "bury the hatchet" or "smoke the peace pipe." A great many Native Americans lost their way of life and the land upon which their ancestors had lived for thousands of years.

Many Native Americans lost their land after the arrival of Europeans in North America.

51

Glossary

A

adobe, n. a type of brick made from sundried clay **(25)**

ancestor, n. a relative who lived a long time ago **(16)**

C

canyon, n. a deep valley between mountains, cut through the rock by river water **(20)**

caribou, n. a species of deer native to North America **(17)**

clan, n. a group of families claiming a common ancestor **(41)**

cliff dweller, n. a person who lives on a rock ledge or cliff wall, such as a member of the Ancestral Pueblo people **(20)**

confederacy, n. a loosely organized group of states or tribes **(38)**

council, n. group of people who meet to help run a government **(40)**

E

ebb, v. to move away from the shore **(48)**

F

fuel, n. a substance that is used to create heat or energy **(19)**

G

game, n. animals that are hunted for sport or for food **(33)**

H

herd, n. a large group of animals that live and travel together **(5)**

hide, n. an animal's skin **(17)**

hunter-gatherers, n. small groups of people who feed themselves by hunting animals and gathering plants **(5)**

I

Ice Age, n. a period in Earth's history when huge sheets of ice covered large parts of Earth's surface **(2)**

ice sheet, n. a very thick piece of ice that covers a large area of land for an extended period of time **(2)**

igloo, n. a dome-shaped temporary shelter made from snow blocks **(18)**

L

land bridge, n. a small strip of land that connects two large land masses **(2)**

landscape, n. the physical features of an area **(44)**

longhouse, n. large, rectangular dwelling with doors located at each end and places for fires inside **(47)**

M

mammoth, n. a large, prehistoric elephant-like animal covered with hair **(5)**

mastodon, n. a large, prehistoric animal similar to an elephant and a mammoth **(12)**

mesa, n. from the Spanish word for table, a rocky, flat–topped hill **(32)**

mineral, n. a naturally occurring substance found in Earth's crust **(26)**

mound, n. a large, rounded pile **(27)**

musk ox, n. a wild ox with a shaggy coat and downward curving horns **(5)**

N

northern lights, n. soft, colorful light that appears in the sky in northern lands, caused by the reflection of sunlight **(14)**

P

peace pipe, n. a ceremonial pipe used by Native Americans **(51)**

Pueblo, n. a group of Native American people who live in the American Southwest **(23)**

R

river valley, n. an area of low land surrounded by mountains and hills, often with a river running through it **(12)**

S

sachem, n. a chief in a Northeastern Native American nation **(49)**

soil, n. the top layer of Earth's surface where plants grow **(13)**

spear, n. a long, thin weapon made from a pointed stick, sometimes with a stone or metal tip **(6)**

stalk, n. the thick stem of a plant **(46)**

symbol, n. a picture or object that is a sign for something; for example, the American flag is a symbol of the United States **(42)**

W

wigwam, n. a domed dwelling made of poles tied together with bark covering the sides built by the Eastern Woodlands people **(47)**

Core Knowledge®

CKHG™
Core Knowledge HISTORY AND GEOGRAPHY™

Series Editor-In-Chief
E.D. Hirsch, Jr.

Editorial Directors
Linda Bevilacqua and Rosie McCormick

Subject Matter Expert

Jeffrey Hantman, PhD, Department of Anthropology, University of Virginia

Illustration and Photo Credits